Publish a Book!

Compare over Fifty
Self-Publishing Companies

J. Steve Miller

Cover photo by Svetlana Braun, purchased from istockphoto.com. Cover design by Chenboi and Carole Mauge-Lewis

For corrections, book orders, bulk discounts, author appearances, inquiries or interviews, contact publisher by email or regular mail:

Wisdom Creek Press, LLC 5814 Sailboat Pointe NW, Acworth, GA 30101

www.wisdomcreekpress.com

ISBN-13: 978-0-9818756-6-8

Wisdom Creek Press, LLC

DEDICATION

For Cherie - my partner in life, love and publishing.

CONTENTS

Preface
So You Decided to Self-Publish!

It's okay. Really. I've been traditionally published and had a wonderful experience. I've also self-published and enjoyed this experience tremendously. I've sold lots of books both ways. From my experience, it's not that one method is inherently better than the other. Rather, traditional publishing is better for certain authors and certain books and self-publishing is better for others. It's really that simple.

This book assumes you've decided to self-publish, so I won't discuss the pros and cons. Neither will I discuss what it takes to actually sell your book. (I talk about both in my earlier book, *Sell More Books! Book Marketing and Publishing for Low-Profile and Debut Authors.*) Just remember that choosing the best self-publishing company doesn't guarantee that you'll sell any books. Many self-published authors, even those widely distributed through the best companies, seem to sell no books at all once their closest relatives, friends, and loyal employees have purchased copies. But to be fair, most debut and low-profile *traditionally* published authors don't sell many books either. Typically, the books that sell well in either sphere are by authors who write great books and market them with equal doses of savvy and passion.

Although finding the right company is only one ingredient to publishing success, it's a critical one that can make or break your hopes of publishing a quality, successful book. I pray that this book helps you to make the best choice for that essential ingredient.

J. Steve Miller

Introduction
Why This Comparison?

You've written a manuscript and want to self-publish. So out of the hundreds of companies competing to transform your words into a book, which should you choose? Does it really matter? Don't they all simply print books, produce e-books, and place them in the main selling channels, offering similar services and charging similar fees that must be kept low to compete with rival companies?

You'd think so, but I hear a steady stream of authors pouring out their horror stories of how their publishing companies ruined any chance they had of success. Ignore those warnings to your peril.

"Can't I Just Skip to the Comparison Charts?"

Sure, but you'll likely misinterpret them if you lack the necessary background information. The charts merely compare a few prices and features; but which features are the most important for your book and which price differences matter most?

Trust me. If you want people to read your books, you need to understand the industry that prints your books and gets them out to the public. Master these details and you'll find yourself way ahead of most authors.

So if you're serious about writing books, block out the necessary time, prepare a cup of your favorite tea, and think through the options that could make or break your book.

Why Trust Me?

First, I have no insider connections. I don't work for any of these self-publishing organizations. Neither am I being paid by someone in the industry to promote a certain viewpoint.

Second, I'm not out to publish you or sell you my services. Although Cherie (my wife) and I created our own publishing company, we currently use it to publish our own books exclusively.

Third, I don't have a personal ax to grind with any of these publishers. My personal experiences have been good, both with traditional publishing (published by Tyndale House and Standard Publishing and several international publishers) and self-publishing (through CreateSpace, Amazon's Kindle Direct Publishing, Barnes & Noble's Pubit, Smashwords, Android App and iPhone App).

Fourth, I have a high tolerance for detail. A reviewer once called me a dogged researcher, which means I can be of assistance to authors who want to understand publishing options without having to agonize over the small print on scores of websites, make numerous phone calls for clarification and read thousands of relevant customer experiences on blogs, forums and listservs.

My Approach

Cherie and I love to write and plan to continue writing for the rest of our lives. But since ignorance can spell doom in this rapidly evolving field, we knew that we needed to understand the business side of publishing. If you want to simply write for the sake of writing, then keep a diary. But if you want others to read your work, you'd better understand today's publishing options. As someone well said,

> "In times of profound change, learners inherit the Earth, while the learned find themselves beautifully equipped to deal with a world that no longer exists."

Here's what jolted me into turning my research into a book.

After writing *Sell More Books*, fellow authors began to ask in more detail about publishing options, often recounting heart-wrenching stories of how companies had ruined any glimmer of hope they had for success. The dreams they nurtured during years of research and writing were dying because of publishing commitments that guaranteed minimal sales.

This past summer, fellow author/publisher Eddie Snipes and I offered free publishing advice from a booth at America's largest independent book festival – The Decatur Book Festival – in Atlanta. As we talked to writers, we felt the weight of their confusion over publishing. Their passion was the written word, or their story or their subject matter, not studying publishing options; they just wanted to get their work out there. So after spending years perfecting their manuscripts, they probably searched "self-publishing" in Google and found several companies promising everything they needed: an effortless process, professional editing, fantastic design, and even publicity following publication.

They were assured that these companies could deliver because the company websites were filled with glowing testimonies of satisfied authors. Perhaps the sites were even sprinkled with Bible verses and a bit of Jesus talk to assure authors of their sincerity. But Jesus himself warned us to beware of wolves in sheep's clothing. Many authors report that once they handed over their money:

- The representatives who promised to hold their hands throughout the process were apparently busy holding other people's hands.
- Authors were required to set exorbitant retail prices on Amazon that nobody in his right mind would pay, effectively guaranteeing failure in the marketplace.
- The services they paid $5,000 for were actually worth much less or could have been obtained free of charge.
- They couldn't get out of their contracts to place their manuscripts elsewhere.
- Author copies were much too expensive to purchase in mass, yet they needed inexpensive author copies to mail for review and to sell locally.
- They couldn't access timely reports of sales. As a result, they couldn't determine which of their marketing efforts were actually producing sales.

So study publishers with a critical eye. As King Solomon warned, the naïve believes everything, but the prudent considers his steps. If you're serious about a company, study the contract carefully. Call or e-mail to clarify important details. Google each publisher's name to discover what authors *currently* say about them. Companies can change quickly, particularly in this quickly evolving industry.

Additionally, Google phrases such as "(publisher's name here) complaints" or "(publisher's name here) sucks." Critically evaluate "customer" praises and criticisms. Sometimes dissatisfied authors were lazy or inept and are looking for someone to blame for their second rate books. Other times, employees of unscrupulous publishing companies may pose as disgruntled authors to slam their competition. So enter the fray with your eyes wide open. The naïve don't fare well in publishing.

If you believe I've missed the mark or misrepresented a company, please let me know at jstevemiller@gmail.com. I typically provide web addresses to the appropriate sites to allow you to check my facts and figures, but links change over time.

* * * * * * *

Clarification: "Printers" or "Publishers"?

Should people refer to Lightning Source (LSI), Create-Space (CS), and the rest of the self-publishing service companies as "printers" or "publishers?" Some insist on calling LSI a "printer," since LSI neither designs nor edits. But LSI does much more than simply print books. They take book orders for author copies, ship books, keep records, distribute to major wholesalers, and cut checks for the proceeds – all services traditionally associated with publishers.

Some call CS a "Subsidy Publisher" or "Vanity Publisher,"

since they offer optional paid services such as design and editing. Yet, many authors bring their edited and designed manuscripts to CS and use none of the extra paid services.

Many of these companies offer the option of publishing your manuscript as an e-book. To me, expanding the word "printer" to include producing e-books stretches the already extended word beyond recognition. Pay words overtime when you work them that hard.

Thus, in my humble opinion, these strict distinctions confuse more than clarify. All these companies 1) are popularly referred to as publishers and 2) fit my dictionary definition of "publish": "to print and issue to the public." Technically, I could say that "I'm publishing my book through my own publishing company (Wisdom Creek Press), outsourcing to CreateSpace my printing, shipping, record keeping and distribution to major retailers." But adherence to such distinctions makes for clunky writing. To keep things simple, I'll sometimes refer to myself as publisher and at other times refer to these publisher service companies as publishers.

Chapter One
Compare Lightning Source (LSI) and CreateSpace (CS)

Hopefully, this approach will simplify matters greatly. LSI and CS presently reign as two of the most popular and respected leaders in print on demand (POD) publishing. Even if you choose a different publisher, traditional or nontraditional, understanding what these companies offer will help you to make an informed choice. In fact, most (if not all) of the self-publishing service companies I mention will publish your book through either LSI (most likely) or CS. Learn what these two offer and you'll have a base line to compare the services and costs of other companies. In some cases, you'll discover that some of the "services" that other publishers charge for can be obtained free of charge elsewhere.

Both companies print tons of books. By mid 2010, Create-Space surpassed publishing two million book titles, CD titles and DVD titles. Lightning Source has been used by over 20,000 publishers. When other companies claim to be "the leading self-publishing company" (several do), compare these figures.

Most experienced self-published authors that I communicate with on forums and listservs (e.g., the Yahoo *Self Publishing Group*) recommend self-publishing through CS and LSI, except in special cases. These two behemoths can typically print and distribute your book with the optimum combination of the:

- least expense
- most potential profit
- highest quality
- least hassle

I said *typically* because there are always exceptions. If you've written a full-color children's book, which tends to be pretty expensive through print on demand, consider pricing a printer in another country who could print a couple of thousand copies pretty inexpensively. If you want to produce a small number of books, or a portfolio of your graphic artwork, one of Lulu's specialty tracks may streamline the process and offer the special binding that you want. Each self-publishing company claims to offer something special – a niche in the market that makes them the best choice for certain authors with certain books. Our first responsibility is to determine whether that niche is real or illusory in your case, then to determine if the rest of the package is a good or bad deal for authors.

But let's hold off comparing other companies until we've looked more closely at CS and LSI. Comparing many companies at once in a vast chart can be confusing and even misleading because it's difficult to compare apples with apples in this industry.

Similarities between CS and LSI

- Both are great companies with many raving fans. I wouldn't say that one is *better* than the other; one may simply be better *for you* than the other.

- Both can distribute your books through Ingram and Baker & Taylor, the largest and most important wholesalers for bookstores, libraries, Wal-Mart, etc.
- Both can get your books onto Amazon.com and BarnesandNoble.com – the dominant online book-sellers.
- Both allow you to check your sales at any time you'd like via their sites.
- Both charge extremely low upfront fees.
- Both allow authors a large percentage of each sale (royalties.)
- Both allow authors to keep all their rights, so that authors can republish anywhere else they choose.
- Both offer affordable author copies for giveaways, promotions, and local sales.
- Both produce quality books.

Basic Differences

1. LSI works exclusively with publishers. CS works with both individuals and publishers, but caters to individual authors. Practically speaking, even if you're self-publishing your first book, you can probably still publish through LSI. Simply register a unique publishing company name (not named after yourself!) through your county or state; buy your own ISBN numbers through Bowker

http://www.bowker.com/index.php/identifier-services/book-title-identifiers-isbn

in the name of the publishing company you just started, and finally look in a mirror and say to yourself, "I am a publisher!'" (It wouldn't hurt to put up a website for your company.) Now that you're a publisher, sign up on the LSI site

http://www1.lightningsource.com/new_client.aspx

with your company name and your ISBNs and they'll typically (they can accept or reject you) welcome you as a publisher. It's really that simple.

****

Recommendation: Establish Yourself as a Publisher

No matter which of the scores of self-publishing companies you choose to publish through, if you hope to sell many books to the public, I recommend that you establish yourself as a publisher so that when your book is published, it doesn't appear self-published (your name listed as publisher) or vanity published (CreateSpace, for example, listed as publisher).

Many reviewers and buyers routinely dismiss books that are either self-published or published by a known vanity (author pays to publish) press. While that may seem unfair, serious reviewers and buyers don't typically have time to shuffle through a million self-published books when they assume that books published through traditional publishers provide more consistent quality control.

****

2. LSI doesn't offer cover design, interior layout, editing, or marketing packages. Publishers either do those in-house or pay others for those services. Bring to LSI your finished book in digital form and they'll print and distribute it through the main wholesalers.

3. LSI includes distribution through Baker & Taylor, which many libraries order from. CS also offers distribution through Baker & Taylor, but only if you use a CS ISBN number. I prefer to use my own ISBN so that the publisher associated with our books is Wisdom Creek Press, LLC (our publishing company) rather than CreateSpace (which would identify the book as self-published).

4. CS offers optional services such as cover design, interior layout, editing, and marketing.

CS can either function solely as your printer/distributor, or do the work of a subsidy (vanity) publisher. If you go with CS, should you pay for their extra services? It's up to you. If you know great editors within your writers' group who'll edit one another's manuscripts free of charge, why pay CS? If you know a great graphic artist that you trust, why not go with her? Just make sure to give her all the specifications that CS lists for cover art for the size book you've chosen.

Does CS do quality work with their extra services? I typically hire people I know and trust to do these services, but I'd check with customers on forums who used CS to discover their experiences. My CS contacts have always dealt with me in a very personal and professional way. As I write, they also guarantee their services. If you pay them to do a cover design and you're dissatisfied with the final product, report it within 60 days and they promise to refund your money.

Much of what we deem as excellence in design work is in the

eye of the beholder. Thus, working with any designer can be a challenge and you'll probably find both satisfied and dissatisfied customers of CS design and editing.

Cost to Publish

If you bring your edited and laid out manuscript, plus your cover design, in the appropriate digital formats, here are your costs to print and distribute through CS and LSI:

CreateSpace Cost to Publish

It's free to publish. (In 2012 CS consolidated its Pro Plan and Standard plan into one, free plan for all.) Did you read what I just wrote? FREE! "But what if the book's 600 pages?" FREE! "But what if it contains tons of words in tiny print?" FREE! "But don't I have to pay a yearly fee to keep it listed?" I said FREE, FREE, FREE!

Now if you're reading these words as a child prodigy or an adult suffering from long-term memory loss, you may lack the historical perspective to fully appreciate the impact of free publishing. Prior to quality print on demand technology, publishers typically had to print 3,000 to 5,000 copies to get the price per copy low enough to compete in the marketplace. That could mean $6,000 to $10,000 in printing costs, before you could sell your first book! Initial printing costs made publishing a high-risk venture.

With quality print on demand (POD) technology, individual books can be printed one at a time as they're ordered, drastically reducing initial publishing costs and revolutionizing publishing in the process.

Today, if you're fascinated with niche topics like growing eggplants or raising weasels, you can write a book about your passion and publish free of charge. Even if nobody outside of your close relatives and best friends and a niche group of weasel lovers want a copy, you've not lost money in the process. (If you're serious about free publishing, you'll want to marry a great editor and raise a graphic artist. It worked for me.)

I've not digressed here to chase a rabbit. In my opinion, some of authors' greatest publishing mistakes are made by assuming that quality publishing costs big bucks. Thus, they're taken in by the publishing company that promises to "do it all" for $10,000.

Typically, for a 300 page book, if I feel I need outside help, I may pay someone $300 to do a final edit (after extensive personal editing and input from friends and family) and pay a professor of graphic design $300 to design my cover. Many authors get by with much less. If your layout is pretty simple (no fancy formatting), you can probably lay it out yourself in Microsoft Word (as I did with this book).

So if CS and LSI publish so cheaply, how do they make a profit? While CS makes some money on their optional services, both use print on demand technology and take a portion of the sale of each book.

Although CS automatically makes your books available on Amazon.com, I recommend purchasing the "Expanded Distribution" for $25.00 (one-time fee) to get on Barnes & Noble and to allow other bookstores to order through wholesalers/distributors such as Ingram and

NACSCORP.

Lightning Source Cost to Publish

$75 one time setup fee per title + $30 for each proof copy. Pay a $12.00 per year catalog fee per title to maintain the listing.

Bottom Line on Initial Cost to Publish: Although Create-Space is a bit cheaper, both are very reasonable.

Author's percentage (Royalties) of Each Amazon Sale

LSI and CS have potentially significant differences here, leading some authors to strongly prefer one or the other. Both companies are very straightforward about how they pay authors. When someone purchases your book on Amazon, Amazon keeps part of that money, then LSI or CS takes their cut, which pays for printing your books, taking orders, shipping, credit card fees, keeping records, customer service, etc. Goodbye to the days when self-published authors had to store thousands of books in the basement, take orders, wrap and ship books, and keep all the records. Now we can concentrate on writing, publishing and marketing!

So what do you receive each time one of your 200-page books, with a 6" by 9" trim size, full color cover, and black and white interior sells on Amazon for $16.00?

Author Royalties on Amazon Sales with CreateSpace

You receive $6.35 per copy sold.

[CS figures this by taking the price you list on Amazon.com and subtracting 1) 40 percent of the list price 2) a fixed charge

($2.15 for a book of 24 to 108 pages; $0.85 for a book of 110 to 828 pages) 3) and a per page charge ($0.012 per page for books 110-828 pages.)]

* * * * * * *

For the latest specifics on royalties from CreateSpace, check here:

https://www.createspace.com/Products/Book/Royalties.jsp

Their royalty calculator allows you to put in the details (list price, trim size, number of pages) and calculate your royalties:

https://www.createspace.com/Products/Book/#content5

* * * * * * *

Author Royalties on Amazon Sales
With Lightning Source

You can choose your discount. (CS, by contrast, sets all Amazon sales at the 40 percent discount.)

- **With a 20 percent discount, you receive $9.30.**
- **With a 40 percent discount, you receive $6.10.**
- **With a 55 percent discount, you receive $3.70.**

So why would an author choose a higher discount and receive less money per sale? Because some authors prioritize trying to get their books into brick and mortar bookstores, which typically won't stock books unless they can purchase them at the standard 55 percent discount. Other authors don't prioritize brick and mortar bookstore sales, so they choose a smaller discount so that they'll receive more for each

Amazon.com or Barnes & Noble.com sale. Even if you choose a 20 percent discount, people can typically *order* your book through a traditional bookstore; just don't expect bookstores to *stock* it since it wouldn't be profitable for them.

Comparing Royalties beyond Amazon

If your book sells on BarnesandNoble.com or through Ingram to a bookstore, CreateSpace pays you $3.15, with no options for varied discounts, compared to LSI's above royalties, based upon the percentage discount you choose. (Again, we're assuming a 200 page book, selling for $16.00.) Lightning Source is the clear winner here.

The 20 Percent Discount: A Big Advantage for Lightning Source

For many authors, the 20 percent discount is the main reason they publish through LightningSource. If you're mainly concerned with Amazon sales, then receiving $9.14 per book at the 20 percent discount significantly trumps CreateSpace's $6.21. With the 20 percent option, if you sell 1,000 books through Amazon, you make $9,140 with LSI, compared to $6,210 through CS. That's close to a $3,000 difference! (CreateSpace does have its own store separate from Amazon.com, so that authors can link to it from their author sites and get the 20 percent discount in this way. But typically sales come through Amazon.com rather than the CreateSpace store.)

Caveat to the LSI "Big Advantage"

This past summer (2011, updated October 13), self publishing expert Aaron Shepherd reported that "we can no longer count on good availability on Amazon for books distributed through Lightning Source."

(http://www.newselfpublishing.com/PlanB.html).

Here's the problem, which changed everything for many authors/publishers. Even with print on demand, many books must be printed and warehoused by Amazon, resulting in both space and logistical limitations.

Whatever the reasons, many authors who published through LSI no longer saw their Amazon listings labeled "in stock." Rather, they were listed as available in 1-3 weeks. This was an obvious turn off to many buyers, negatively impacting sales. Thus, some Lightning Source authors began to publish additionally with CreateSpace to ensure "in stock" status on Amazon. They kept their LSI accounts as well, but changed their settings to not sell through LSI to Amazon.

Of course, this ruins their strategy to get a 20 percent discount on Amazon. Since Amazon planned to open new warehouses, the policy might be reversed, but even then publishers need to be aware of this potential downside to publishing solely through LSI.

Cost for Author Copies

From my experience, my books are my most useful tools for marketing. Especially if I want to send out multiple copies for review, the cost of author copies matters. If I can purchase 200 author copies for $4.00 each, I pay $800. At $8.00 each, I'd pay $1,600. The price of author copies is also critical for making money off back of seminar or local sales.

Lightning Source offers author copies of a soft cover, 6" x 9" book, black and white interior, color cover, 212 pp. for $3.66 per copy (not including shipping), offering discounts for orders over 100 copies.

CreateSpace offers author copies of the same book for $3.39 per copy, plus shipping.

(To make an accurate comparison, compare both companies for your book's specific dimensions and page length and the number of copies you're ordering.)

Distribution and Sales Channels

Both CS and LSI put you with the two largest wholesalers: Baker & Taylor and Ingram. Both put your book on Amazon.com and Barnesandnoble.com. Baker & Taylor is favored by many libraries. Ingram is the primary wholesaler to traditional bookstores.

Note: Older forum entries often say that CS distributes only through Amazon. But within the last two years, CS began distributing additionally through the most important wholesalers, Ingram and Baker & Taylor.

Insider Advantages?

Be aware that since LSI is a subsidiary of Ingram, this privileged relationship may give them some advantages over books published through LSI. Similarly, since CreateSpace is a subsidiary of Amazon.com, CS books may have some advantages with Amazon. Here are three examples.

1. Members of a marketing forum recently informed me that Amazon was doing something new: allowing authors to

request by e-mail a few key words (not the same as "tags") to help readers find our books on Amazon. I went to my "Author Central" pages on Amazon.com, but saw nothing about this. How were authors supposed to find out about this important feature?

Before I e-mailed Amazon to make the request, I checked my CreateSpace account and found that I'd already submitted my keyword requests when I submitted my book to them. It was simply on one of the standard forms that I'd completed in the publication process. So in this case, many authors with other publishers may never learn about this feature, whereas CreateSpace authors would have routinely taken advantage of it.

2. As I mentioned above, this past summer Amazon listed many LSI books as available in one to three weeks, rather than in stock. Apparently, this didn't happen to CS books. Again, the Amazon/CS connection paid off in an unexpected way.

3. Some authors have reported that LSI books are quicker to get onto Barnesandnoble.com than CS books. One author wrote her book on a very timely topic and wanted to beat her competition to Barnes & Noble, so she published through LSI to get it there more quickly.

So, because of their business alliances, there may be very real differences between LSI and CS in distribution and sales that surface from time to time. This is a fast-moving industry and companies are quick to try new strategies. Check your fellow authors' up-to-date experiences on the appropriate listservs and forums. (See my recommended resources section.)

Determine which sales channels are most important to you and take them into consideration when choosing a printer/publisher.

ISBNs

You can use CreateSpace's free ISBN or purchase your own through Bowker. If you go with LSI, you'll have to purchase your own through Bowker. I purchase my own ISBNs so that my publisher's name follows it wherever it's sold. Again, I don't want to look self-published, because of the current stigma.

Ease of Use for Authors

CreateSpace typically wins here, since Lightning Source, catering to publishers, assumes you have the knowledge of an experienced publisher. CS's instructions spell out what to do in pretty simple terms, although getting a cover image into just the right format and just the right dimensions can be a bit daunting the first time around. Some things about publishing, even when simplified, aren't that simple. Welcome to publishing!

CS also offers a forum (not offered by Lightning Source) where authors can discuss issues with experienced CreateSpace authors. You can also either call or e-mail your representative free of charge. My representative, John Mark Schuster, has always proven very knowledgeable, patient, and calls or e-mails back within 24 hours of my contact.

I've heard of both CS and LSI authors who were either ecstatic about their publishing contacts or didn't find them very helpful. In my opinion, your representative can be pretty critical to your having a good experience. If you don't hit it off, try to work things out. But if you just don't fit, request another one. There are plenty to go around.

Summary of CreateSpace Versus Lightning Source

CreateSpace is set up to deal with authors. Lightning Source is set up to deal with publishers. Typically, individual authors will be happier with CS and publishers will be happier with Lightning Source. Both are good companies and most authors and publishers I hear from are happy with customer service. It's no small accomplishment that only three people have lodged complaints with LSI at the Better Business Bureau over the past three years, and one with CS. Each of these complaints were responded to by the companies. This is quite remarkable for companies that deal with tens of thousands of creative people.

Reviews and Customer Experiences with LSI and CS

Here are some useful places on the web to find information on LSI and CS. [Please note that although the Better Business Bureau (BBB) is a helpful place to find how many complaints have been lodged against a company and how many of the complaints have been resolved, its ratings (A+, A, A-, B+, etc.) seem to be impacted by whether or not the company has chosen to pay for membership with the BBB. Many good companies choose not to pay, and this decision often negatively impacts their ratings. For more information on the Better Business Bureau, see Appendix #3.]

Posts Comparing LSI and CS

Aaron Shepherd uses both companies and gives the best

and most up-to-date comparisons I've found.

http://www.newselfpublishing.com/blog

Reviews and Customer Experiences with Lightning Source

Better Business Bureau on Lightning Source (listed under their parent company, Ingram):

http://www.bbb.org/nashville/business-reviews/barge-lines/ingram-industries-in-nashville-tn-10701 .

A Thread on Absolute Write about Lightning Source:

http://absolutewrite.com/forums/showthread.php?t=1 26574

Self-Publishing Review on Lightning Source:

http://www.selfpublishingreview.com/blog/2011/06/li ghtning-source-review

On Complaints Board:

http://www.complaintsboard.com (search for Lightning Source)

Reviews and Customer Experiences with CreateSpace

Better Business Bureau on CreateSpace:

http://www.bbb.org/western-washington/business-reviews/storage-units-household-and-commercial/create-space-self-publishing-in-seattle-wa-22643410 .

Independent Review of CreateSpace:

http://mickrooney.blogspot.com/2009/02/createspace-reviewed.html

CS Forum (customers freely ask questions, complain, and post responses.)

https://www.createspace.com/en/community/index.jsp a

Review on Self-Publishing Review:

http://www.selfpublishingreview.com/blog/2011/09/createspace-usa-review

On Complaints Board:

http://www.complaintsboard.com/complaints/createspace-c230123.html

So now you understand what two of the industry leaders offer authors. You've made major progress! Now you're in a much better position to evaluate other companies.

Chapter Two
Compare E-Book Publishing Options

But before we make these comparisons, let's look briefly at e-book options, since e-book sales are becoming increasingly important to authors – in many cases eclipsing their paper book sales. As I write, Amazon is selling more e-books than paper books. Overall in the book industry, e-books represent 14 percent of consumer fiction and nonfiction sales.

With the following overview, you'll learn how you can publish e-books directly through the same avenues that publishing companies use.

With e-books all the rage, it's important to optimize our e-book distribution and royalties. Many self-publishing companies offer e-book services, either as an add-on, or automatically bundled into a package. To decide if it's a good idea to pay a company to publish your e-book, compare your company's offer (initial costs, e-book royalties, yearly fees), with the deal you get by publishing directly with the main sellers/distributors of e-books.

Authors who hold the rights to their books, know their way around Microsoft Word, and have the patience to follow detailed instructions can publish their own e-books with wide distribution through the main channels absolutely free of charge. Those who don't want to do it themselves can pay individuals to do it for them without having to go through a self-publishing company.

It's free to publish an e-book for Kindle.

Open an account with Kindle Direct Publishing here:

https://kdp.amazon.com/self-publishing/signin

After you've formatted and submitted your manuscript per the instructions, your e-book will be available on Amazon (including Amazon sites for the US, UK, Canada, Germany, Austria, France, Italy, Vatican City, San Marino, Spain, Andorra, and expanding rapidly). Authors receive 70 percent (if priced between $2.99 and $9.99) of the Amazon selling price. Your Kindle e-book can be read on "Kindle devices and Kindle apps for iPad, iPhone, iPod touch, PC, Mac, Blackberry, and Android-based devices." Authors can track their sales on a daily basis and are paid monthly.

It's free to publish an e-book for Barnes & Noble's Nook.

Register on the PubIt! site here:

http://pubit.barnesandnoble.com/pubit_app/bn?t=pi_reg_h
ome

Format it according to their instructions and it will be listed for sale on the Barnes & Noble site. Note that there are minor differences in formatting for Kindle and Nook. Authors receive 65 percent of the selling price on B & N if the e-book is priced between $2.99 and $9.99. Sales can be checked each day and royalties are paid monthly.

It's free to publish for other e-stores and e-readers (e.g., Apple's iBookstore, Sony Reader's Store, Kobo and the Diesel eBook Store).

I use **Smashwords** to get my e-books with these other stores, since it's either difficult or impossible to publish to them directly:

http://www.smashwords.com/about/how_to_publish_on_
smashwords

* * * * * * *

Update 1/10/13

Some authors give Amazon exclusive sales of their e-books, at least for a time, so that they can give away free copies through Amazon's KDP Select program. By offering them for a couple of days free, books often get high rankings in a genre or category and get into enough readers' hands that word of mouth results in increased sales. For this reason, some authors may format their e-books only for Kindle, at least initially.

* * * * * * *

It's typically more difficult to format for Smashwords, since they're formatting for several e-book platforms simultaneously. You can do it all in Microsoft Word, so there's no programming involved. The Smashwords instruction manual walks you through the process step by step.

Authors receive 60 percent of the list price set by their major retailers. I set my Smashwords books to **not** be distributed to Barnes & Noble and Amazon, so that I get my full 70 percent or 65 percent royalties on those channels, since I registered directly with each of them.

I've often used one of Smashwords' unique features for marketing. Authors can set up coupon codes for discounts, so that when they're seeking reviews, they can link reviewers to their book on Smashwords, allowing reviewers to download it free of charge for a limited time period in the format they prefer (for Kindle, for Nook, in pdf, etc.). It sure beats mailing out review copies! This feature also allows authors to give a discount (e.g., 30 percent or 50 percent or 100 percent) for special promotions.

Is the E-book Add-On with Self-publishing Companies a Good Deal?

Many self-publishing service companies offer e-book publishing services. Here are your main considerations.

1. Compare the author royalties you'll get if you pay your self-publishing company to format and distribute your e-books. If they offer a percentage of their "net," ask them to translate that into "When my e-book sells for $9.99 on Amazon, how much money ends up in my pocket?" Get it in writing or (better) find it spelled out on their site.

2. If you don't want to fool with formatting, there are many freelance formatters you can hire. Mark Coker, founder and president of Smashwords, will send you a list of reasonably priced formatters if you e-mail list@smashwords.com.

3. For marketing purposes, it's important (and fun!) to track our daily sales. As I do a marketing campaign, I like to know immediately if book sales are spiking. If your publishing company publishes your e-book, will you be able to track daily sales on Barnes & Noble and Amazon?

4. Using coupons to sell e-books is great for special campaigns ("50 percent off this week only!") or for giving away copies to reviewers. Can you use this feature on Smashwords if your self-publishing company publishes your e-book?

Recommendation: If you can't tolerate details and have the money to hire it out, compare prices of several experienced e-book formatters who can put your book directly up on Amazon (as a Kindle), Barnes & Noble (as a Nook) and Smashwords. But if you're saving money and/or want to publish more books in the future, go ahead and learn to format it yourself. If your book is in Word format and isn't that complicated (no complicated interior artwork, text boxes, etc.), it's really not that difficult.

So now you can better evaluate the e-book services offered by self-publishing companies. Additionally, you're acquainted with two of the industry leaders in print on demand publishing – Lightning Source and CreateSpace. Armed with this information, you're much better equipped to understand and evaluate what other publishing companies offer.

Chapter Three
Clarify Fuzzy Language
And See through Outright Deceptions

So what about the hundreds of other companies competing to publish your book? I'm not suggesting that Lightning Source and CreateSpace are the only good companies. Since each self-publishing company claims to fill a niche and offer something special, each probably has its strengths and weaknesses. By understanding LSI and CS, you're in a better position to evaluate those strengths and weaknesses.

"So can't I skip on down to the charts?" you may ask. Not so fast. Stop fidgeting. Stand up. Take a break. Pour yourself another cup of tea. Here's where the claims of competing companies gets confusing. Many published authors are kicking themselves today because they didn't take the time to learn the fine art of "publisher speak" and failed to understand the implications of accepting various terms in their contracts.

After obsessing on scores of company websites and reading thousands of customer experiences on independent sites, I think it's critical for authors to familiarize themselves with some commonly misunderstood claims and definitions that often appear in this industry. Without this understanding, authors can read entire company sites and study comparison charts while completely missing the red flags that should be popping up all around.

When researching a company, *thoroughly* answer these four basic questions:

1. Does the company offer better prices than CS and LSI for the same quality of features and services?

2. If a specific service costs more, are they offering more value for that extra money?

3. Do their customers generally report (on independent sites, blogs, forums and listservs) satisfaction with these companies?

4. Does the company offer extra services or features that neither CS nor LSI offer?

Let's look at these questions one at a time.

Question #1. Does the company offer better prices than CS and LSI for the same quality of features and services?

I've seen up front prices range from free to well over $10,000.

Self-publishing service companies typically use Lightning Source (most likely) or CreateSpace to publish their books. So if they must pay Lightning Source the same price that you'd have to pay, they must charge authors more for *something* in order to make a profit. Perhaps you're paying for editing, cover design, and interior layout, which Lightning Source doesn't offer. That would be legitimate. But whatever the case, **know how they're making their money and precisely what you're paying for.**

Understand all the initial ("set up" or "package" charge, charges for proofs and last minute changes, etc.) and ongoing charges (annual "listing fee" or "cataloguing fee"), comparing them carefully with LSI and CS. Typically in business, if all other matters are equal, it makes better business sense to cut out the middle man and go straight to the main suppliers.

If a company charges the same initial fees as LSI and CS, which are extremely low, then where do they make their money?

- **Do they require you to set a high retail price for your books, so that they make more money on each of your sales?** Many companies assume that self-published authors will sell copies to only a small circle of friends and family, who would be willing to buy an overpriced book because of the relationship. If this is a company's approach, the high retail price will almost certainly hinder your sales to people outside of your friends and family. I know authors who are bound by contract to accept their company's exorbitant retail price, which effectively kills their sales.

- **Do they charge authors more for author copies, hindering your ability to make a profit when you sell at local events and limiting how many you can purchase to send for review and special promotions?**

- **Do they charge more for shipping, so that the listed price for author copies isn't the whole story?**

- **Do they take a higher percentage of each sale that could be going to the author?**

- **Do they charge a large yearly fee to keep your book catalogued and distributed?** I e-mailed one company to ask for their annual fees, which they failed to mention on their site. For authors to keep their author website, e-commerce, listed with wholesalers, etc., they would have to pay over $800 per year per book!

* * * * * * *

Clarification: Royalties Based on the "Net" Versus the "Retail"

Some companies figure royalties by a percentage of the "net" (e.g., a percentage of what the company receives from Lightning Source) whereas others figure royalties by a percentage of the retail price (e.g., its selling price on Amazon). This can make a huge difference. Cut to the chase by asking (and getting in writing), "If my book sells for $10.00 on Amazon.com, how much money ends up in my pocket?"

Example: Let's say that your $10.00 book sells on Amazon. Your self-publishing company might receive 30 percent of that sale, or $3.00. If your self-publishing company gives authors 50 percent of the "net," you'll receive 50 percent of that 30 percent, or *15 percent of the retail price. $1.50 ends up in your pocket.*

* * * * * * *

Question #2: If a specific service costs more, are they offering more value for that extra money?

Publishing companies are full of promises. But can they deliver? One company claims to specialize in getting their books into bookstores. So I called some of the largest bookstores to see if they would order from this company. They said no, because the company was obviously a vanity publisher (pay to publish).

Beware of expensive marketing services offered by publishing companies. From my research, (see details in *Sell More Books!*), sending out a press release to 10,000 media outlets (unless this is a cultivated, individualized list, which is unlikely) will likely sell no books at all, unless your book tackles an extremely timely topic that the media might swarm to. Most of these services can be done either free of charge or much more inexpensively than through a self-publishing company. If you're serious about selling your books, study book marketing and discover what you can do yourself.

Charges for such services as cover design, layout and editing can be compared quite easily. More difficult is determining up front if they are a pleasure to work with and if their work will be done professionally and on schedule. Read independent forums and complaint sites to get candid customer feedback on such services.

And remember, if you go with CreateSpace, you don't have to use their added (for pay) features. Some authors find editors through their writers' groups and cover designers through a local college (professor or gifted student). Connect with fellow authors through forums and local writing organizations to discover who's talented, reasonably priced, and easy to work with.

Question #3. Do their customers report (on independent sites, blogs, forums and listservs) satisfaction with these companies?

I read many authors posting on forums, "How I wish I'd visited this forum before I chose a publishing company!" Of course, don't believe every comment. But after reading customer experiences on multiple forums and blogs, you get a feel for what's accurate and what's bogus. As King Solomon said, "in an abundance of counselors there is victory." I share many links below to forums, listservs and blogs, where you can learn from an "abundance of" customer experiences.

Question #4. Does the company offer extra services or features that neither CS nor LSI offer? For example, if you want a picture book or portfolio, neither CS nor LSI may offer the binding or easy set-up tools you'd like to use for your specific book.

Tips on Comparing Publishing Companies

Expanding upon the above four questions, here are some specific suggestions as you compare.

1. Dig beyond the front page information on "initial cost to publish" and "ease of publishing." After spending years writing their masterpieces, authors are itching to see their book in print. So they look at a comparison chart showing one company with an initial cost as cheaper than another, including customer testimonials saying the process was insanely easy and customer service was great. They conclude,

"Why shop around? This company offers what I want at a price I can afford. Let's get this baby out there!" But please, shop around. With publishing, critical issues often hide in the details.

2. Author copy costs can make a huge difference. So one company prices author copies at $4.00 a copy and another company at $8.00. "So what's the big deal with a $4.00 difference? How many author copies do I need anyway?" If you plan to sell books to the public, probably a lot. From my book marketing experience, my most effective advertising piece is my book. Book marketing guru John Kremer suggests that successful book marketers typically send out hundreds of free copies for review. I'm much more likely to give out $4.00 books than $8.00 books.

3. Even small price differences can make a big difference. Book selling often succeeds or fails by small margins of profit. Expanding upon the last point, I'll give an example. This month, an acquaintance proposed purchasing bulk copies of my book, *Sell More Books!*, and reselling them when he teaches seminars. To make it worth his while, I want him to make a decent profit off the sales. To make it worth *my* while, I needed a bit of profit myself. Since I get copies of my 332 page book at about $5.50 per book (including shipping), I can purchase copies in bulk from CS and have them shipped directly to him. If he pays me $8.00 per book, I make $2.50 per book and he can make $4.00 per book selling them for $12.00 per book, beating the Amazon price so that attendees are motivated to purchase at the seminar rather than wait until they get home to order elsewhere.

With this arrangement, everybody wins. I make a profit; the seminar leader makes a profit; seminar attendees get a discounted book. **But if I had to pay as little as $2.50 more for each author copy, I'd make no profit at all with this arrangement.**

To reiterate: Small differences in charges can make a huge difference in your ability to sell books.

4. Price your book too high and it won't sell. Some companies force authors to sell their books for ridiculously high prices. Bookstore managers know that customers won't purchase a $19.95 mystery from an unknown author when they could buy a $12.95 mystery by Sue Grafton. Don't be surprised if bookstores won't carry your overpriced book and if potential readers pass you by.

5. Shipping costs can be a deal breaker. Yet, these costs aren't typically spelled out on the public pages of company sites. Ever gotten ripped off by finding the best deal for a product online, only to discover in the last step of ordering that the exorbitant shipping charges make it the absolute *worst* deal? Understand shipping and handling costs *before* committing to a company!

Also, know which countries your company mails from. If you live in England and your company prints only in the USA, you'll be paying international postage to get your proofs and your author copies. A Canadian author reported on a blog that to get one, $12.00 book shipped from her USA based publishing company to Canada cost her $89! Just try selling your book for $89! Another publishing company would have charged $12.00 for the same service!

Example: LSI currently has printing facilities in the USA, Great Britain, France and Australia. They may have more by the time you read this!

http://www.ingramcontent.com/newsroom_detail. aspx?id=327

6. Beware of the misleading language that permeates this industry.

While some companies appear straightforward, others would have been described by the late Lewis Grizzard as "slicker than a bucket of greased eels." Look for the following phrases and decipher their clever nuances of meaning.

- "We're the leading self-publishing company…."

  Many of these companies claim to be the "leading" or "top" self-publishing company. But how could they all be "leading"?

  Here's the emotional impact of that statement. If this is the first company you've looked at, the statement leads you to assume that more authors use it than any other company. This in turn spawns the thought: "There's safety in numbers. Why would so many authors be using them if they're ripping people off? Why look any further? I've found the leader!"

  The important part of the sentence is typically the last part, so that one company claims to "lead" self-publishing companies *in making the process easy* (but may offer rotten royalties); another claims to "lead" *in high author royalties* (but sucks at customer service); another "leads" *in company growth* (doubled its output from 20 books last year to 40 this year). To the uninitiated, it appears that each of these is claiming to lead the industry in general (more books, more authors) rather than leading in a specific niche of the industry.

Think about it – perhaps their "graphic artists" can do nothing more than copy and paste an image into a template, but since they're very kind and personable on the phone, they "lead the industry" in customer service!

- "Unlike other self-publishing companies, we're on the side of you, the author."

You'll find this claim frequently – putting down those selfish, money hungry "other companies" and assuring authors that their company is the one that has authors' best interests at heart. If one company offers a decent price on, for example, author copies, they may say, "We don't charge insane prices for authors to get copies of their own books like those *other* companies – how unfair they are to authors!" What they *don't* reveal is that although they do sell author copies at a decent price, they may require authors to set an insanely high price for their books on Amazon, effectively killing sales. *Remember, they've got to make their money somewhere.* If they're not making it in sales of author copies, they're making it elsewhere.

- "Your book will be available nationwide in bookstores."

The key word here is "available," as opposed to

"stocked." Bookstores routinely refuse to stock self-published books. To be fair, any given bookstore must reject the vast majority of *traditionally* published titles as well. They simply don't have room for that many books. Sorry. That's the way it works.

Since most of these self-publishing companies seem to print through LightningSource, bookstores may order your book if someone walks into their store and places an order. That means it's "available in bookstores." But bookstores rarely order selfpublished books to keep on their shelves. It simply doesn't work for their business model.

That's no big deal to me, since bookstores have never been a great avenue of sales for low-profile, not-yet-famous authors. Just remember that phrases like "We distribute through the major wholesalers and a massive network of over 25,000 bookstores" typically means that they print through Lightning Source, which lists their books (like most of the other self-publishing companies) through the largest whole-salers – Baker & Taylor and Ingram. Just don't take this to mean that bookstores will actually order your books to put them on their shelves.

- "We're a traditional publisher."

Remember, traditional publishers pay authors, typically thousands of dollars, for the privilege of publishing them. If companies ask for upfront money, they're not traditional publishers. Sometimes they soften the sentence to "We're a hybrid of traditional and self-publishing." By this, perhaps they're claiming to accept only a small percentage of proposals or to do an exceptional job of getting their books into bookstores. If so, put these claims to the test. Call the decision makers at ten bookstores to see what they know of the company and if they stock their books.

- "We offer authors the highest royalties and best prices for author copies in the industry."

I find multiple companies making the same claims. They can't all offer the best prices. So do your own comparison.

- "We give authors 100 percent of their royalties."

We'll excuse the newbie who imagines that this means that they pay the highest possible royalty. "After all," the newbie imagines, "what company could offer more than 100 percent?" Yet, "royalty" is commonly defined as "the portion that authors receive from the sale of their books." Thus, using the standard definition, *every* author should get 100 percent of his royalties from any publisher he chooses. A royalty is *by definition* 100 percent of the author's portion.

So the useful question isn't, "What percentage of the royalty goes to the author?" but rather "If one of my books sells on Amazon or another channel like Barnes & Noble, how much money from that sale ends up in my bank account?" That's an entirely different question.

Practically speaking, this means that when comparing author royalties, look beyond their confusing percentages.

Now let's take a break to test your understanding of author royalties. Which of the following deals (all of which I've seen on sites) offers the most money to authors?

a. "We offer authors 10 percent of the sale of your book on Amazon."
b. "We offer authors 40 percent of the Amazon sale, but then deduct our expenses for producing the book."
c. "We offer authors 50 percent of our net proceeds on an Amazon sale, defining "net" as the amount of money we make on an Amazon sale."
d. "We offer authors 100 percent of their royalties."

Sorry. Trick question. There's actually not enough information given to decide which is best. For example, how much does company b deduct for expenses? How much does company c make from Amazon? What are the royalties for company d? We simply don't know.

Now do you see how confusing it can be? Don't worry; we'll sort things out for you in the tables below. Just make sure that as you're comparing, always ask specifically how much money you'll receive on a sale of your specific book, listed for a specific price by a specific retailer.

6. Watch for extra fees not spelled out on the main website pages. If a representative gives you a price by phone, ask for a place on the site that spells this out or ask for written confirmation.

On forums, authors complain about companies charging something extra at every turn of the process. You typically find this information by browsing forums, which brings us to the next point.

7. Browse discussions on forums and listservs (see the resources I recommend at the end). Company sites may tell you only what they want you to hear. But on forums, both ecstatic and infuriated customers tell you in detail what happened after they signed on the dotted line. Just remember, older posts (even one year old) often share dated information. Consider reading longer forum discussions that span years from the end to the beginning, so that you're reading the most recent responses first.

Example: Many older posts speak of CS as not offering hardback versions or not distributing outside Amazon or not selling internationally. CS now does all three. This is a fast-changing industry. What was true six months ago may not be true today.

8. Get verbal promises in writing. Better, ask them where you can find it on their site. Several of the representatives I talked to gave me what I later discovered was misinformation. I'm not saying they lied. Perhaps they were misinformed.

9. Typically, paid for, cookie-cutter marketing campaigns are overpriced and do little to sell books. And companies that claim to do a great job of marketing

books should produce solid evidence (beyond a few testimonials) to back that claim. From my experience and research (see *Sell More Books!*), low-profile authors need to study book marketing themselves to determine what will work best with their unique books and personalities. A $500 press release may truly be e-mailed to 5,000 media mavens, but will any of them read the e-mail? And did it result in reviews and sales for the last 500 authors who shelled out the bucks? Typically, nobody collects these statistics. Talk with a number of fellow authors who paid for the service to see how it worked for them.

Chapter Four
Compare Everyone Else

My Approach to Comparing Companies

Again, I'm not telling you which company to go with. I'm simply laying out information to help you make an informed decision. By the time you read this book, some companies may have changed drastically, so that you'll benefit more from my *principles* of evaluation rather than my specific evaluations.

The bottom line isn't always costs and distribution.

- Perhaps you need a special feature that only a few companies offer, such as spiral binding or a special type of paper.
- Perhaps your author buddy had an exceptional publishing experience through a company, and this friend has volunteered to walk with you through the entire process with this company. In this case, this helpful relationship may trump the fact that the initial cost is $500 dollars more than you'd pay at another company.
- Perhaps you're not concerned about costs, so that low author royalties and high purchase costs for author copies don't matter.
- Perhaps you want to sell only to friends and family, so that ordering cheap author copies is your main priority rather than setting a low retail price.

Since I don't know your goals, I simply want to give you the information you need to make an informed decision.

Why am I Comparing Only with CreateSpace?

I'm trying hard to simplify. Since most of my readers are probably authors rather than publishers, it makes sense to compare with CreateSpace instead of LSI, since CS targets authors. (You can always look above to get comparative figures for Lightning Source.) Also, since CS offers additional features, such as cover design and interior layout, this choice allows us to compare these added features as well.

Why Compare only Amazon Pricing and Sales?

Again, I'm trying to simplify. Currently, more people buy books online than in brick and mortar bookstores. Amazon currently dominates the book selling industry, far outselling all other book retailers and growing each year. One survey found 73 percent of their responders buying their books primarily from Amazon.com. A British survey found 80 percent of respondents preferring Amazon.com for their online purchases.

I'll link you to places on each site so that you can compare the latest prices/features yourself. As links change, please let me know so that I can either update this book or indicate changes at www.sellmorebooks.org.

CreateSpace Versus Lulu

According to Lulu, "Since our founding in 2002, 1.1 million creators from more than 200 countries and territories have signed up with us. And each month, we add approximately 20,000 titles to our catalog."

Unless otherwise noted, I'm comparing a 6"x9", 200 page, color cover, black and white interior, paperback book, where the author brings her designed cover with her edited and laid out manuscript. (Compared 10/18/2011. Pricing and features change.)

Service	CreateSpace https://www.createspace.com	Lulu www.lulu.com
Cheapest, No Frills Option to Publish	**Free to publish.** Add a $25 one-time fee to get expanded distribution beyond Amazon.com. If you don't have your own cover design, use their free Cover Creator with templates and your own cover art to do it yourself. You can talk to your author representative to get assistance during the publishing process.	Free, if you want to allow for purchase only on www.lulu.com and Amazon.com. To add distribution through Ingram, sales on Barnes & Noble, etc., upgrade to their Global Reach Distribution for $75.00.
Author Royalty (Amount author receives) on each Amazon sale if list price is $19.99	$8.74	$3.60
Price for Each Author Copy (if you purchase 10 copies and list the	$3.25 + shipping. CS also has a shipping calculator open to the public.	$8.50 for one, $7.65 each for 20, $6.80 each for 100, $5.95 each for 500 + shipping.

book for $19.99)		
Lowest Retail Price you could set for a 218 Page Book	$8.65	$11.72
Annual Cataloguing Fee	No annual fees	No annual fees (verified with Lulu via e-mail).
Rights	Author Keeps Rights	Author Keeps Rights
ISBN	Free CreateSpace ISBN Optional: Bring Your Own ISBN	Free Lulu ISBN with the added Global Reach Distribution. Optional: Bring Your Own ISBN
Cover Design	Hire your own designer outside CreateSpace or do it yourself or pay CreateSpace $349.00 for a custom cover (not template based).	Hire your own designer outside Lulu or do it yourself or pay a designer to do it with a template for $115.00.
Interior Layout	Hire your own designer outside CreateSpace or do it yourself or pay $379.00 for CS to do a custom layout.	Hire a designer outside Lulu or do it yourself or pay $299 for Lulu to do it for you, choosing one of 6 possible layouts.

Considerations

Determine shipping costs (for author copies) to your location to do a fair comparison. Rates vary for different quantities and depending upon which country you're shipping from and to. With both companies going global and offering printing in multiple countries, this can be a critical factor.

While older forum posts mention that Lulu offers the hardback option and CS does not, note that **CS now offers hardback books as well, although they're available only for order by authors, not for sale on Amazon or for distribution through Ingram or Baker & Taylor.**

Advantages of Lulu

1) Lulu offers ways to produce specialized books that CS doesn't currently offer, such as photo books, calendars, cookbooks, yearbooks, wedding books, and portfolios. I know one professor who guides her students to create portfolios of their graphic work on Lulu. Lulu's free design tool, Lulu Studio, allows authors to choose from various themes appropriate for each kind of book. Lulu offers several paper types and bindings (like Saddle Stitch or Coil) appropriate for such books. So, if you're creating a specialty book, check out Lulu's offerings.

2) Having no annual fee is a great deal!

Disadvantages of Lulu

1. For a traditional fiction or nonfiction book, color cover and black and white interior, Lulu offers significantly lower royalties and charges significantly more for author copies than either CS or LSI. (Again, check the cost of shipping, which could make a major difference on author copies, depending upon which country you live in.)

2. Having to set a higher retail price could limit sales.

3. Lulu books sold on Amazon may face the problem of occasionally being listed as available in one to three weeks (not "In Stock").

Lulu Reviews and Customer Experiences

Better Business Bureau on Lulu:

http://www.bbb.org/raleigh-durham/business-reviews/internet-marketers/lulu-enterprises-in-raleigh-nc-90003737

173 complaints over three years, all responded to by Lulu.

Blog post on Lulu vs. CreateSpace vs. Lightning Source:

http://duskpeterson.livejournal.com/49913.html

PC Magazine Review of Lulu:

http://www.pcmag.com/article2/0,2817,2302311,00.asp#fbid=YVgaVdYfhFQ

The Gadgeteer Tests Lulu for creating a photo book:

http://the-gadgeteer.com/2010/10/01/lulu-photo-book-review

Complaints Board

http://www.complaintsboard.com/?search=lulu

RipOff Report

http://www.ripoffreport.com

CreateSpace Versus Xlibris

Xlibis has published over 28,000 titles and has worked with over 25,000 authors. Unless otherwise specified, we'll compare a 6"x9", 200 page paperback book, color cover, black and white interior, where the author brings her designed cover with her edited and laid out manuscript (Compared 10/18/2011. Pricing and features can change.)

Service	CreateSpace https://www.createspace.com	Xlibris http://www2.xlibris.com
Least Expensive, No Frills Option to Publish	**Free to publish.** Add a $25 one-time fee to get expanded distribution beyond Amazon.com. If you don't have your own cover design, use their free Cover Creator with templates and your own stock photos and author pic to do it yourself. You can talk to your author representative to get assistance during the publishing process.	**Advantage Package - $449.00.** Use their free templates; bring your own cover art; do it yourself (but no author representative to help you personally with the process).
Author Royalty (Amount Author Gets Paid) on each Amazon	$8.74	$2.00

sale if list price is $19.99		
Price for Each Author Copy (if purchase 10 and list at $19.99)	$3.25 + shipping. CS also has a shipping calculator open to the public.	$12.99 + shipping.
Lowest Retail Price you could set for 218 Page Book	$8.65 (as listed in my CS members area for one of my books)	$19.99 – Or pay $249.00 extra to set your own price
How Often Pays Author Royalties	Monthly	Quarterly
Annual Cataloging Fee	No annual fees	No annual fees
Rights	Author Keeps Rights	Author Keeps Rights
ISBN	Free CreateSpace ISBN or Bring Your Own ISBN	Free Xlibris ISBN No option to bring your own ISBN
Cover Design	Hire your own designer outside CreateSpace or do it yourself or pay $349 for CS to do a custom design.	Hire your own designer outside Xlibris or do it yourself or pay $225 for Xlibris to do a custom design.

Advantage of Xlibris

1) Savings on cover design. (An advantage only if its quality is comparable to CreateSpace.)

Disadvantages of Xlibris

1) The high cost of author copies can cramp an author's marketing. At $3.25 per author copy (CS price), I'd pay $325.00 for 100 author copies. At $12.99 (Xlibris' price) I'd pay $1299.

2) The high cost of author copies can hurt my ability to profit from local sales. Imagine that a local independent bookstore offers to take your book on consignment, with a typical 50/50 author/publisher split. If it retails for $19.99, then the store would want it for $10, leaving you with a negative profit, since you had to pay $12.99 + shipping for each author copy.

3) The high retail prices (unless you pay the $249.00 to set your own price) can discourage sales.

4) According to the "senior consultant" I talked to at Xlibris, they use their own printers for books that are ordered directly through their Xlibris store; but books ordered outside of Xlibris, such as on Amazon.com, are printed through Lightning Source. Thus, **when Amazon experiences book storage overload, Xlibris books might get the dreaded "shipped in 1-3 weeks" rather than "in stock" treatment.**

5) According to the consultant, authors must use Xlibris' ISBNs, which identifies books as being self-published and makes it extremely difficult to get serious reviews

and attract sales from bookstores. (Go to Xlibris' bookstore, then look up some of their books on Amazon.com, and you'll notice that Xlibris is listed as the publisher.)

Xlibris Reviews and Customer Experiences

Complaints filed with the Better Business Bureau: 289 in the last three years, all responded to by Xlibris, but 38 of the customers considered the resolution unsatisfactory.

http://www.bbb.org/indy/Business-Reviews/publishers-book/author-solutions-inc-in-bloomington-in-32002554/complaints/#breakdown

Complaints Board:

http://www.complaintsboard.com/complaints/xlibris-c402232.html

Pissed Consumer:

http://xlibris.pissedconsumer.com

Rip Off Report:

http://www.ripoffreport.com/book-publishers/xlibris-com/xlibris-com-is-a-scam-dont-wa-e6xm2.htm

Complaint Now:

http://www.complaintnow.com/Xlibris-Corporation-Complaints/complaint/business/Business_ID/display/17831

CreateSpace Versus Outskirts

Unless otherwise noted, we're comparing a 6"x9", 200 page book, color cover, black and white interior, paperback, where the author brings her designed cover with her edited and laid out manuscript (Compared 10/18/2011. Pricing can change.):

Service	CreateSpace https://www.createspace.com	Outskirts Press http://www.outskirtspress.com
Cheapest, No Frills Option to Publish	**Free to publish.** Add a $25 one-time fee to get expanded distribution beyond Amazon.com. If you don't have your own cover design, use their free Cover Creator with templates and your own cover art to do it yourself. You can talk to your author representative to get assistance during the publishing process.	Although their Emerald Package is the least expensive at $199, it isn't comparable to CS because, among other things, this package doesn't allow for distribution (i.e., not available on Amazon). Their Ruby Package is the most comparable, at $699.
Author Royalty (Amount Author Gets Paid)	$3.92 [If we were to compare sales outside of Amazon, Outskirts	Outskirts allows you to choose your discount. At a 25 percent discount (Ruby or

on each Amazon sale if list price is $11.95	would beat CS (if you chose Outskirts' 25 percent discount) since the CS royalty would be $1.53.]	Diamond plans only, not available with the Emerald plan we chose above), author receives $1.80 to $2.80, depending on your package. At a 40 percent discount that comes to $.01 to $1.01.
Price for Each Author Copy (if purchase 10 and listed at $19.95)	$3.25	The percentage discount differs according to the package, with the best discount being 69 percent off retail, which comes to $6.18.
Annual Cataloging Fee	No annual fees.	$25.00 digital storage and hosting fee
Rights	Author Keeps Rights	Author Keeps Rights
ISBN	Free CreateSpace ISBN Optional: Bring Your Own ISBN	Outskirts ISBN included in the Ruby Package. Optional: Pay for your Own ISBN (approved by Bowker, but 20 percent discount)
Custom Cover Design	$349.00	Starts at $299.00

Advantages of Outskirts

1) CreateSpace doesn't offer several features that Outskirts offers, such as a manuscript evaluation, an author website, and ghostwriting.

2) If you purchase your own ISBN through Outskirts, you get a 20 percent discount for your ISBN off what you'd pay at Bowker.

3) Upgrade to the $999 package and you get distribution to the Christian market through Spring Arbor.

4) With certain packages, Outskirts' royalties can beat CS royalties when sales are made outside of Amazon.com. If you plan to primarily sell books outside of Amazon, this could be a factor.

Disadvantages of Outskirts

1) The yearly fee of $25 adds up over time and with more books. An author with four books would pay $100 each year, or $1,000 each decade.

2) Since Amazon sales are typically critical for sales to the public, receiving less royalties on Amazon sales is significant.

3) If you want to sell books on Amazon, you must pay for at least the $699 package. Are they adding significant value for that added expense?

4) Author copies cost almost twice as much, hindering your ability to sell locally, make deals with resellers, and send out copies for review.

Outskirts Reviews and Customer Experiences

Better Business Bureau: 32 complaints in the past three years, all responded to, but 6 customers were not satisfied with the response.

http://www.bbb.org/denver/business-reviews/publishers-book/outskirts-press-in-parker-co-6000433

Self-Publishing Review of Outskirts – note the 30 responses as well.

http://www.selfpublishingreview.com/blog/2009/01/outskirts-press-review

Outskirts' CEO responds to common complaints.

http://brentsampson.com/category/outskirts-press-complaints

CreateSpace Versus iUniverse

Unless otherwise noted, we're comparing a 6"x9", 200 page book, color cover, black and white interior, paperback, where the author brings her designed cover with her edited and laid out manuscript (Compared 10/18/2011. Pricing can change.):

Service	CreateSpace https://www.createspace.com	iUniverse http://www.iuniverse.com
Cheapest Option to Publish	**Free to publish.** Add a $25 one-time fee to get expanded distribution beyond Amazon.com. If you don't have your own cover design, use their free Cover Creator with templates and your own cover art to do it yourself. You can talk to your author representative to get assistance during the publishing process.	$599.00 for the Select plan. But to be fair to iUniverse, this isn't an apples to apples comparison, since this plan contains many extra services, such as custom cover design, formatting for the e-book version, book design and layout, all of which would add to the cost of the basic CS package. Example: A

		custom cover design with CS would cost $349.00 and a custom layout would cost $379.00, *making iUniverse less expensive* in an apples to apples comparison (assuming that the quality of the services are equal.)
Author Royalty (Amount Author Gets Paid) on each Amazon sale if list price is $15.95	$6.32	$2.04
Price for Each Author Copy (if purchase 10 and listed at $19.99)	$3.25 + shipping	$13.99 + shipping
Lowest Retail Price you could set for a 332	$12.43 (based on the lowest price CS allows for my 332 page book.)	$17.95

Page Book		
How Often Pays Author Royalties	Monthly	Quarterly
Annual Cataloguin g Fee	No annual fee	No annual fee
Rights	Author Keeps Rights	Author Keeps Rights
ISBN	Free CreateSpace ISBN Optional: Bring Your Own ISBN	Free iUniverse ISBN

Advantages of iUniverse

1) iUniverse claims to offer authors something between self-publishing and traditional publishing, i.e., "supported self-publishing" – their publishing professionals will guide authors through the publishing process. If their publishing professionals are truly of a higher caliber than the publishing professionals who perform the same functions (e.g., editing, design, marketing, etc.) at other companies, then this could indeed be a qualitative advantage.

2) The $599.00 Select Plan is a good price for the features it includes, such as book layout, cover design and formatting for an e-book. If the quality of these services meet or exceed the quality of CS, then this is a good deal on initial cost.

Disadvantages of iUniverse

1) The author royalty is one third the royalty through CS, which is a major disadvantage to those who hope to sell

books to the public through Amazon. In the royalty example cited, for every 100 books sold, the author makes about $400.00 more by publishing through CS.

2) In the case cited, iUniverse charges four times as much for author copies, limiting the author's ability to send out review copies and to profit from local sales.

3) The royalty on e-books is much less. If you format (or pay someone else to format) your book for Kindle and submit it to Kindle yourself, Kindle publishes it free of charge and authors receive 70 percent of the selling price on Amazon. If your e-book is published through iUniverse and a copy sells on Amazon, you receive 50 percent *of their net*. This means that you take the price charged by Amazon, first subtracting the "channel discount" (which may be 50 percent, depending upon the discount you choose), and the author takes 50 percent of what remains, which is equal to 25 percent of the retail. So an author who published a $10.00 book directly through Kindle would receive $7.00 in royalties on each Amazon sale. Published through iUniverse, the author (with the 50 percent discount) would receive $2.50 for each Amazon sale.

4) Authors may have the problem of occasionally being listed on Amazon as "available in one to three weeks."

iUniverse Reviews and Customer Experiences

The Better Business Bureau lists iUniverse under their parent company, Author Solutions, which has 289 complaints over the past three years. While Author Solutions tried to resolve the complaints, 38 of the complaints were not resolved to the satisfaction of the customers.

http://www.bbb.org/indy/business-reviews/publishers-book/author-solutions-inc-in-bloomington-in-32002554

Complaints Board

http://www.complaintsboard.com/?search=iuniverse&everything=Everything

Pissed Consumer

http://www.pissedconsumer.com/?option=com_search&Itemid=38&searchword=iuniverse&go=

RipOff Report

http://www.ripoffreport.com

CreateSpace Versus Xulon

Xulon targets Christian authors writing Christian books, emphasizing their "100 percent royalty rate paid to authors for all bookstore sales."

Unless otherwise noted, we're referring to a 6"x9", 200 page book, color cover, black and white interior, paperback, where the author brings her designed cover with her edited and laid out manuscript (Compared 10/18/2011. Pricing can change.):

Service	CreateSpace https://www.createspace.com	Xulon http://www.xulonpress.com
Cheapest, No Frills Option to Publish	**Free to publish.** Add a $25 one-time fee to get expanded distribution beyond Amazon.com. If you don't have your own cover design, use their free Cover Creator with templates and your own cover art to do it yourself. You can talk to your author representative to get assistance during the publishing process.	$1,299 – This includes a custom cover, layout, and a few additional items not offered in CreateSpace's least expensive options.

Author Royalty (Amount Author Gets Paid) on each Amazon sale if list price is $15.99	$6.34	$3.30
Price for Each Author Copy (if purchase 10 and listed at $15.99)	$3.25	$10.39
Lowest Retail Price you could set for 332 Page Book	$12.43 (based on the lowest price CS allows me for my 332 page book.)	$18.99
How Often Pays Author Royalties	Monthly	Quarterly
Annual Cataloguing or Renewal Fee	No annual fees.	$29.95
Rights	Author Keeps Rights	Author keeps rights.
ISBN	Free CreateSpace ISBN Optional: Bring Your Own ISBN	Free Xulon ISBN comes with package.
Custom Cover Design	$349.00	Included in package
Custom Interior Layout	$379.00	Included in package

Advantages of Xulon

1. For no extra charge, they add your book to Google Book Preview. Although any author can do this personally, free of charge, it's a time saver to have someone else with experience to do this for us.

Disadvantages of Xulon

1. It appears that you must use a Xulon ISBN, identifying authors as self-publishers and making it difficult to get serious reviews and sell in bookstores.

2. The $29.95 per year "renewal fee" is pretty hefty. If I had five books with Xulon, I'd pay about $150 per year or $1500 per decade just to keep them listed and for sale.

3. The required retail price is typically above the market rates, hindering sales.

4. Paying three times as much for author copies discourages buying large numbers to send out for review and makes it difficult to make money selling copies locally.

5. Lower royalties on Amazon sales hurts author profits.

6. The packages seem very expensive, unless there's added value somewhere that I'm not seeing.

Customer Experiences with Xulon

1. Customer Complaints with the Better Business Bureau:

http://www.bbb.org/central-florida/business-reviews/publishers-book/xulon-press-in-longwood-fl-163747420/complaints - of 22 complaints registered, 9 customers were not satisfied with Xulon's response.

2. Author testimonials at Xulon:

http://www.xulonpress.com/success_stories.php

3. Largest thread of comments I've seen about Xulon - almost 300 comments by their customers on an apparently neutral site:

http://www.topix.com/forum/business/radio/TFFK5QMV 3PR4CFSLA#comments

4. Article about a customer experience, with other customers adding comments.

http://www.associatedcontent.com/article/414929/publishi ng_beware_of_christian_claims.html?cat=38&com=2

5. One Xulon customer's experience, with 20+ replies

http://www.associatedcontent.com/article/405168/xulon_pr ess_author_warns_beware_do.html?cat=38

4. Complaints Board:

http://www.complaintsboard.com/complaints/xulon-press-longwood-florida-c328867.html

Other Publishers

By this point, you should know what to look for in a self-publishing company, how to interpret various words and phrases, how to evaluate claims, and when to ask clarifying questions. So, for the following companies, I'll limit myself to brief synopses, linking you to further information. Additionally, please note that *I'm limiting myself to information I can actually access on their sites*, rather than relying on personal e-mails and conversations with representatives, which are more prone to error or dispute.

Example: one company said nothing on their site about any ongoing yearly fees, so I don't mention it below. But when I e-mailed for clarification, they replied that authors would have to pay over $800 per year, per title, to retain many of their features such as extended distribution, a website, etc.

Lesson: if you're interested in any of the below companies, look past the websites and read the contracts thoroughly before signing anything!

Apples to Apples?

By quoting the example prices given by each company, I've prioritized accuracy over comparability. Thus, you'll find an example of a royalty based on a 200 page book for one company and a 311 page book for another, depending on the example they used.

Royalties as a percentage of the Net

Reminder: When a company figures its royalties as a percentage of the net, we can't calculate the actual author royalty without knowing the percentage discount they've set with Amazon *and* the amount they may be deducting for their printing costs. Thus, the company offering authors 100 percent of their net may actually pay a smaller royalty than the company offering 70 percent of their net. It all depends upon how they figure their net, which is sometimes laid out clearly on their sites and other times is not.

What We're Comparing

All books compared have a color cover with a black and white interior. Companies often offer discounts for larger orders of author copies, but I compared their cost for a single copy, which is typically the same per copy as their price for up to ten copies.

I define "least expensive package" as the cheapest package that includes distribution to Amazon and other basic features that most authors need.

And remember: keep comparing with CreateSpace, Lightning Source and the other above companies, since I don't repeat their details below.

Aachanon Publishing

- Least expensive package = $195.00 (includes template cover design and interior layout).
- Calculate the author price by choosing the retail price for your book and subtracting a "base price" set by Aachanon. Example: Set the retail price of your 200 page book at $14.99. Subtract the "base price" of $4.50 so that your author copy price is $10.49 per

copy, plus shipping, although shipping is free for ten or more books.

Abbott Press (A division of Writers Digest)

- Least expensive package = $999.
- Author royalty = 50 percent of Abbott's net. Example: Your book sells for $17.95 on Amazon. Abbot gives Amazon a 48 percent discount. If the cost of printing is $4.97, then Abbott receives $4.36 (Abbott's net) and you receive 50 percent of that net, which is $2.18.
- Author copies can be purchased at a 30 percent discount, which means that if your book sells for $10.00 on Amazon, you could purchase copies from Abbott at $7.00 each, plus shipping.

Advantage Books

- Their Silver Package is the least expensive at $1,299.00, which includes interior layout and a choice of five templates for a cover design.
- Authors receive 30 percent of the publisher's net.
- Authors receive a forty percent discount on author copies (a book selling on Amazon for $19.99 could be purchased for $11.99 + shipping + $5 handling charge.).
- A 200 page book would retail for $14.99.

An Author's Dream

- Least expensive package = $695.00.

- Royalties = "Twenty-five percent (25 percent) of the sales actually received by the Publisher from any and all sales of the printed Work."
- Author copies available at 35 percent off the retail price. Thus, an author of a $14.99 book could purchase it for $9.70 + shipping.

Arbor Books

Arbor claims to specialize in ghostwriting, editing, cover design, typesetting, printing and marketing. I can't find pricing information on their site. Fill out a form on their website to get a quote.

Ardith

- Least expensive package = $399.00 (use templates for cover and interior layout).
- Royalties = 40 percent of their net.
- $100 per year to maintain the book file.

AuthorHouse (According to the Better Business Bureau, Author House is one of many subsidiaries of Author Solutions, including Wordclay, iUniverse, Inc., Xlibris, Trafford Publishing, Balboa Press, Westbow Press, Legacy Keeper, Palibrio Author Learning Center, Abbott Press, and Inspiring Voices.

- The least expensive package is the Foundation Package ($599.00), which includes a cover design, interior layout, and formatting for an e-book.
- Royalties on e-book sales = 50 percent of their net. If Author House receives 70 percent of a Kindle sale,

the author would receive 50 percent of that 70 percent, or 35 percent. On the sale of a $10.00 e-book, the author would receive $3.50.

Aventine Press

- Basic service is $399.00.
- Royalties: "A reader purchases a copy of your 160 page book at Amazon.com - The cover price of your book is $12.95; subtract Amazon's 55 percent trade discount ($7.12), then subtract the printing cost ($3.30), and the remainder ($2.53) is the profit margin, 80 percent of which ($2.02) is the royalty paid to you."
- Purchase author copies at "the current printing cost plus 10 percent, plus the actual shipping and handling charges." For a 200 page book, that comes to $3.90 (printing cost) + .39 (10 percent) = $4.29 + shipping.

Balboa Press (a division of Hay House)

- Least expensive package = $999 (includes cover and interior layout).
- Purchase author copies at 30 percent off the retail price. Thus, if your book sells for $10.00 on Amazon, you could purchase it for $7.00 + shipping.
- Author royalties = 50 percent of Balboa's net. Example: Your $17.95 book sells on Amazon. Amazon takes a 55 percent retail discount. If Balboa's printing cost is $4.97, then Balboa receives $3.11 (Balboa's net) for the book, of which you receive 50 percent, or $1.56.

Book Country

- Book Country is owned by Penguin Group, one of the largest book publishers in the world.
- Least expensive package = $299 (for both print and e-book formats; use their tools to do your own interior layout and follow their tips to do your own cover design).
- Author royalties for Kindle sales on Amazon = 70 percent of Book Country's net. If your $2.99 e-book sells on Amazon, the author gets $1.47, since Amazon takes 30 percent of an e-book sale.

Book Locker

- Least expensive package = $517.00 (includes formatting and cover design), or $317.00 if you submit your own cover.
- Minimum retail price for 200 page book: $13.95.
- Royalties on Amazon: 15 percent of list price.
- Annual file hosting fee: $18.00.
- Cost for author copies (for a 148 page paperback listed at the minimum list price): 35 percent off the list price. Thus, the author of a 148 page book listed for $12.95 could buy copies for $8.42 plus shipping.

Bookstand Publishing

Basic package: $299.00 (includes interior layout template and choice of cover templates).

Royalties: 10 percent on Amazon sales. If your book sells for $10.00 on Amazon, you receive $1.00 in royalties.

Author copies: $6.95 per copy + shipping for a 6"x9", 200 page book that retails at $15.95 (minimum order of 25 books).

CCB Publishing

- Royalties = 50 percent of net proceeds.
- Basic package = $750.00.
- Price for author copies = It costs $3.90 to print a 6" x 9" 200-page book. Add their $2.00 fee to make it $5.90 for each author copy. Add shipping.

Dellarte Press

- Targets writers of women's fiction and romance.
- Least expensive package = $599.00 (includes simple layout, standard cover [templates], and formatting for e-books).
- Royalties: For a 175 page book listed at $11.99 on Amazon, the author receives $1.21. (Figured as follows: From the $11.99, subtract 48 percent for their retail discount, then subtract $3.81 for printing cost to get Dellarte's net. Authors receive 50 percent of Dellarte's net.)
- Author copies. 30 percent off retail. Thus, if your book sells for $10.00 on Amazon, you'd pay $7.00 for each author copy, plus shipping.

Dog Ear Publishing

- Least expensive package: $1099.00 (includes custom interior layout and cover design).

- Author copies of a 200 page book are $5.28 each, plus shipping.
- If your book costs Dog Ear $6.03 to print, is offered to Amazon at a 40 percent discount, and retails on Amazon for $14.95, the author royalty = $2.94 per book.

DragonPencil

- Specializes in children's and young adult books.
- Basic package: $987.00 (includes interior design, cover design, formatting for e-book.)
- Royalties: $7.00 author profit for selling a 24 page children's book retailing at $15.95 on Amazon.
- Annual fee: $59.00 for renewal of on demand printing; $49 to continue offering as an e-book.

E-BookTime

- $395.00 for basic package (includes formatting for e-book).
- Royalties on paper books are 15 percent of the retail price on Amazon. For the sale of a $10.00 book, the author receives $1.50.
- Royalties on e-books are 50 percent of the retail price on Amazon.
- Annual cataloguing fee of $12.00 for books that didn't have at least $100.00 in sales over the past year.
- Price for author copies. $9.06 + shipping for a 200 page book.

Epigraph Publishing Service

- Basic package: $899.00 (includes layout and cover design).
- Royalties: Since each author can set her own discount and retail price, these decisions impact the royalties. Their example is a 120 page paperback selling for $15 at a wholesale discount of 40 percent, which would give the author $4.06.
- Annual renewal fee: $35.00.
- Cost of author copies: $6.94 + shipping for a 120 page book.

Equilibrium Books

- Based in Australia, they give some quotes in Australian Dollars (AUD).
- Base package for medium length novel = USD $303.10.
- Retail price for 200 page book = AUD $25.95.
- Royalties = 13.5 percent of the sale price.
- Up to 40 percent discount for author copies.

Foremost Press

- Least expensive package = $347.00 (which includes a light edit and typesetting.)
- Retail price for a 200 page book = $13.97.
- Royalties on print versions = 50 percent *of net receipts*.
- Royalties on e-books are determined by subtracting 97 cents as a transaction cost and paying authors 50 percent of what remains.

- Authors can purchase copies at 50 percent of the retail price.

Fultus Publishing

- Least expensive package = $449.00 (includes interior layout and choice of templates for cover).
- Author copies offered at a 40 percent discount. Thus, if your book sells for $10.00, you get copies for $6.00 + shipping.
- Author royalties are 15 percent of an Amazon sale ($1.50 for a $10.00 book).

Global Authors Publications

- Least expensive package = $2,000 (includes interior layout, cover design, and editing for spelling and grammar).
- Yearly fee = $150.
- Author copies of a 312 page book: $5.60 (printing cost) + $1.50 (per order) = $7.10 + shipping.

Infinity Publishing

- Least expensive package = $499.00 (includes interior formatting and cover design. Add $199.00 for distribution through Ingram and Baker & Taylor in order to get on Amazon, Barnes & Noble, etc.).
- Author royalties for print books = 15 percent of the retail price on Amazon. This means that a book sold for $10.00 on Amazon would give the author $1.50.

- Author royalties for e-books = 70 percent *of their net*. The author's take of a Kindle sale for $9.95 on Amazon would be $4.87.
- Author purchases = 50 percent off retail for your first order and 40 percent off for subsequent orders + shipping.

Inkwater Press

- Least expensive package = $999.00 (includes interior layout and cover design).
- Author royalties = up to 50 percent of their net. A book selling for $14.95 on Amazon with a 50 percent royalty would give the author $2.49.
- Author copies are offered at a 40 percent discount from the retail. Thus, a $10.00 book could be purchased by the author for $6.00 + shipping.

Inspiring Voices (a service of Guideposts)

- Least expensive package = $699 (includes custom cover and interior design).
- Author royalties = 50 percent of Inspiring Voices' net. If your book sells on Amazon for $17.95, 55 percent would be deducted for Amazon's discount. If the cost of printing is $4.97, then Inspiring Voices would receive $3.11 (their net), of which the author would receive 50 percent, or $1.56.
- Author copies can be purchased at 30 percent of the retail price. Thus, if your book sells for $10.00 on Amazon, you'd pay Inspiring Voices $7.00 per copy + shipping.

Llumina Press

- Least expensive package = $799 + $150 for distribution through Ingram (includes custom cover and interior layout).
- Author royalties = 10 percent of list price. Thus the author royalty on a book selling for $16 on Amazon would be $1.60.
- Author copies for a 200 page book selling at a 40 percent discount on Amazon for $11.95, the author cost is $8.37.

Mill City Press

- Least expensive package = $1497 (includes cover design and interior layout).
- Author royalties for a 200 page book (retailing for $14.00 set at a trade discount of 40 percent through Amazon.com) = $4.50.
- Author copies for a 200 page book = $3.90 + 4.5 percent credit card fee + shipping (for your first order). For subsequent orders, add a $23 administrative fee per order.

Omniland Books/Skyline Publishing

- Least expensive package = $785 (includes cover design and interior formatting)

Omega Publications

- Basic package = $1,050 (includes basic editing, cover design, interior layout).
- Royalties = 80 percent of their net; 28 percent royalty on Kindle sales.
- Author copies = 5 percent more than their cost + shipping.

New Book Publishing/Reliance Media

- Least expensive package that puts your book on Amazon = $1157 (includes custom cover and custom interior design).

Palibrio

- Specializes in Spanish publications.
- Least expensive package that puts your book on Amazon and Ingram = $599 (use cover templates and interior design templates to do it yourself).
- Author royalties = 50 percent of Palibrio's net. Example: One of your books sells for $17.95 on Amazon. Amazon gets 48 percent of the sale. If the printing cost is $4.97, then Palibrio receives $4.36, of which the author receives 50 percent, which comes to $2.18.
- Author copies = 30 percent discount. If your book is listed at $10.00 on Amazon, you'll pay $7.00 per author copy.

Polished Publishing Group

- Located in Canada
- Author royalties: 20 percent of the selling price on Amazon, which means a book selling for $10.00 on Amazon would give the author $2.00.
- Author copies: purchase at a 55 percent discount off the selling price. Thus, a book selling for $10.00 on Amazon could be purchased by the author for $4.50 + shipping.

Press Forward

- Located in Canada.
- Setup cost for a 200 page book = $370.00.
- Suggested retail price = $15.95.
- Author copies = $6.38 + shipping.
- Annual catalogue fee = $20.00.

Publish America

- Author copies = 20 percent discount. Thus, if your book sells for $10 on Amazon, order author copies for $8.00 + shipping.
- Author royalties are calculated as a percentage of Publish America's net.

Qoop

- Niche = several types of bindings, including wire and saddle stitch; regular books and photo books, emphasizes selling via social networking, affiliate sales, etc.

- Author copies of a 200 page book = $10.00 + postage.

Red Lead Press

- Least expensive package = $295.00 (includes interior layout and template cover).

Rosedog Books

- Least expensive package = $980 (includes custom cover, interior layout, and formatting for e-book).
- Author royalties = $1.20 for a $10.00 book sold on Amazon at a wholesale discount of 40 percent.
- Author copies = 40 percent off the retail price, thus a book selling on Amazon for $10 could be purchased by the author for $6.00 + shipping.

Spiderwize

- Located in the UK. (All prices in UK pounds - £.)
- Least expensive package = £549 (includes interior layout and custom cover).
- Author copies for a 200 page book = £3.15 + postage. "The above retail example is based on the author receiving around £1 per book sold with retail discount of 40 percent (the amount of discount given to wholesale / retailers). This retail pricing is only to give you an idea, you are not bound to the above retail settings."

- Annual charge = £15 to keep the book in distribution.

Spire Publishing

- UK and USA (Price quotes in Canadian Dollars).
- Least expensive package = CDN$699.00 (do your own cover design and layout).
- Author copies = CDN$8.95 + shipping for a 200 page book.
- Author royalties = "Retail price $10.99 deduct trade discount of 30 percent ($3.30) = wholesale price of $7.69. With an author price of $6.95 (200 page count or less) this will leave you with a profit, per book sold via the book trade, of $0.74. The above is for calculation purposes only, you can, of course, set the retail price to your liking as long as print costs are covered."

Star Publish LLC

- Least expensive package = $1,000.00 (includes interior design and custom cover.)
- Royalties = 50 percent of their net.
- Author copies = 30 percent above print cost + shipping.

Tate Publishing

- Purchase author copies at a 60 percent discount. A book selling on Amazon for $10 could be purchased for $4.00 + shipping.

- Royalties = 15 percent.

Trafford Publishing

- Least expensive package = $599 (includes layout, cover, e-book formatting).
- Author royalties on paper books = Either 10 percent or 20 percent of Trafford's net, depending on your "Author Selected Royalty percentage".
- Author royalties on e-books = 50 percent of Trafford's net.

UniBook

- Has both USA and Belgium offices.
- Free to publish through their book wizard. (Books available only through their online bookstore.)
- Author royalties = £3.14 if you price your 200 page book at £13.62 and choose to get a 30 percent royalty.
- Author copies = 5 percent reduction in the price of your book if you buy 10 copies.

Unlimited Publishing, LLC

- They charge no upfront fees.
- They "focus on tightly targeted specialty markets more than general interest...."
- They are selective and prefer "short nonfiction books by professional writers."

Virtual Bookworm

- Least expensive package = $360 (includes generic cover).
- Author royalties = 50 percent *of Bookworm's net receipts.* That gives the author $1.15 per book for a 200 page book selling for $10.99 at a 30 percent discount on Amazon.
- Author copies = for the first order, pay 50 percent off the list price + shipping. For subsequent orders, pay 30 percent off the list price + shipping.

Volumes

- Located in Canada
- Least expensive package = CDN$1,699 (includes layout and cover design). (Note: The CDN$799 package didn't include availability on Amazon.)

We-Publish.com

- Least expensive package = $998 (includes cover design and interior layout).
- Author royalty for books *sold through the We-Publish bookstore*: 60 percent.
- Author royalty for e-books (Kindle) = 50 percent.

WestBow Press

This division of the largest Christian publisher, Thomas Nelson, was started in partnership with Author Solutions.

- Packages start at $999 (including interior layout and cover design).
- An author would receive $1.56 in royalties from a $17.95 book sold on Amazon.
- Buy author copies of a $17.95 book for $12.57 each (30 percent off the list price for 1-24 copies).

Wine Press Publishing

- Least expensive package = $1,499 (includes typesetting and two hours of cover design).
- Author royalty for Starter Package = your $17.99 retail book on Amazon pays a royalty of $.54.
- Author copies = 62 percent off retail. Thus a book selling for $10 on Amazon could be bought by the author for $3.80 + shipping.

WingSpan Press

- Least expensive package = $499 (includes color cover and interior layout).
- Author royalty for paper books = 20 percent of the retail price (what it sells for on Amazon). If your $10.00 book sells a copy on Amazon, you get $2.00.
- Author royalty for e-books = $4.20 for the sale of a $9.95 Kindle; $1.50 for the sale of a $5.95 Kindle.
- Author copies = 50 percent of the retail price. If you price the book at $10.00, you get copies for $5.00 each + shipping.

Word Association Publishers

- Least expensive package = $1,200 (includes cover design and interior layout).

WordClay

- Least expensive package = $245.

Conclusion

Since companies change, make sure to research the latest on their sites. Now that you know the language of self-publishing and the main features to compare, you should be well equipped to make wise choices. Whoever you go with, read the fine print, get thorough answers to all your questions, and check the web for customer experiences.

Note the following appendixes, the first being a checklist of essential questions to ask self-publishing companies. The second helps you to evaluate their marketing claims, since many companies claim that their competitive edge is aggressive marketing. The final appendix suggests places to get more information.

Let me know (jstevemiller@gmail.com) your suggestions for making this resource clearer and more up to date, including corrections or any new self publishing companies we should add.

To learn more about writing and selling books, check out our award-winning *Sell More Books! Book Marketing and Publishing for Low Profile and Debut Authors*, and other books at the end of this book.

Keep up with us through our blog

www.enjoyyourwriting.com

and our sites:

www.sellmorebooks.org and www.wisdomcreekpress.com

Appendix 1
Check List
Essential Questions for Publishers/Printers

Service and Quality

___ Search the company in Google for customer complaints.

___ Check common complaint sites such as listed in Appendix #2.

___ Examine books they've published.

___ Get candid input from authors who have used the company.

o Did they meet deadlines?
o Were they courteous?
o Were there bad (or good!) surprises after you began working with them?
o Would you recommend them to other authors?
o Were they upfront with you?
o Was the publishing process easy to navigate?

Initial Cost to Print/Publish

___ Is the price comparable to others in the industry?

___ Will the book be designed (cover and interior) with a template, or from scratch with a totally custom design? Do you like the covers and interior designs for other books they print?

___ Are their claims for extensive distribution actually

a mere list of what everyone gets through Lightning Source and/or CreateSpace?

Binding

___ Do they offer any specialty bindings that you need? (coil, saddle stitch, etc.)?

___ If you want hardback copies, do they offer them either as author copies or for distribution?

___ Do they offer the size you want?

Author Copies

___ Can you purchase copies inexpensively?

___ How much do they charge for shipping and handling?

___ Do you have to purchase in bulk?

___ Are there discounts for bulk ordering?

Instructions and Setup

___ Are the instructions clear?

___ Do they offer professional and courteous phone support?

___ Do they offer a forum or knowledge base for additional knowledge and insider tips?

Rights

___ Do authors hold all the rights?

___ Will you have the right to stop your relationship with them at any time?

___ Will you have the right to republish however and whenever you want?

___ Are you obligated to publish future works with them?

ISBNs

___ Do you provide your own ISBN, or is it provided?

___ If you want the book listed in your publishing company's name rather than theirs, do they allow you to do this by using your own ISBN?

Additional Fees

___ Are you aware of all annual fees, such as "maintenance fees" or "listing fees"?

___ Are you charged extra each time you send back a version of the layout or cover design that was unacceptable?

Business Questions

___ How long has the company been in business?

___ If the company is owned by another company, what is the reputation of the parent company?

Author Royalties

___ Is the method of determining royalties perfectly clear? (Example: "How much money will I get if my

150 page book sells for $10.00 on Amazon?")

___ Are the royalties comparable to such companies as CreateSpace and Lightning Source?

___ How much money do authors need to make before a check is cut?

___ How often are royalties paid?

Printing

___ Is it printed on demand, offset, or digitally?

___ Is the company using its own printers or outsourcing to another company?

___ Are you satisfied with the quality of printing in other books they publish?

Distribution

___ Will it be available through the main wholesalers – Ingram and Baker & Taylor?

___ If you're hoping to have it carried in bookstores, are you able to offer it with a 55 percent discount and a return policy?

___ If you want to get higher profits per sale by selling to Amazon at a 20 percent discount, does the company allow this?

___ If the company does not print through CreateSpace, are you risking not being listed as "in stock" on Amazon?

Retail Price

___ Will their minimum required retail price allow you to sell the book at a price that people are willing to pay?

___ Should you decide to sell an e-book at a very low price, like 99 cents, to spur sales, will they allow it?

Tracking Sales

___ Will you know which channels (Amazon, etc.) your book sold through?

___ Will you know which sold as e-books and which as traditional books?

___ Will you know how many sold on any particular day or week? (So that you can evaluate marketing effectiveness.)

___ Can you check sales daily online?

___ How often will you get reports?

Appendix 2
Evaluate Marketing Claims

Some companies claim to set themselves apart from other companies by aggressively marketing your books. Yet, marketing doesn't necessarily yield results. From my experience, sending out a press release or putting up a book website doesn't by itself tend to yield any sales at all. So is there any way to know if paying a company $500 or $1,000 extra for their marketing efforts likely to yield results?

Let me suggest an informal, but possibly enlightening test. If a company claims that they're better at marketing books than other companies, go to the company's online bookstore, or their list of published books, and find the corresponding titles on Amazon.com. (To compare fairly, search random copies in a single genre rather than their list of bestsellers.)

I selected 10 books from a company that claims to aggressively market their books and checked them on Amazon.

On the plus side, nine were listed "in stock," (although one listing warned that only one was in stock). The title not listed "in stock" was listed as "usually ships in 1 to 4 weeks," indicating the nagging problem that sometimes surfaces on Amazon with companies that print through Lightning Source.

On the negative side, their Amazon pages weren't optimized, even on the most basic level, for success. Most had not activated "Search Inside," the only way to allow customers to browse a few pages. Seven had no reviews at all. The remaining three had only one review each. Yet, getting multiple reviews is one of the main keys to selling books on

Amazon. (One survey found 88 percent of responders saying that they liked to read at least one review of a book before purchasing it.)

A book's Amazon ranking is a significant indicator of sales. Four of the 10 had no ranking at all, which means that nobody has bought a copy on Amazon, ever. (All 10 were listed as at least six months old – some had been listed for multiple years – so we can't attribute zero sales to a slow start.) Four others had rankings ranging from two million to five million, indicating extremely poor sales. Of the remaining two, one showed a decent ranking (426,000) and the final one a great ranking (88,761), showing that those two were getting some regular sales.

Admittedly, ten books is a rather pitiful sampling, but it suggests one way to check sales and compare with the sales of another company. It's always possible that authors sell massive amounts of books through venues other than Amazon, such as after seminars. But if word of mouth is catching on at all, eventually it should result in Amazon sales. Unless a company gives another objective way to evaluate their claims, this may be the best we can do.

Appendix 3
Helpful Links for Further Study
Secondary Sources Comparing
Self-Publishing Companies

While it's helpful to line up scores of companies in columns, comparing their costs and benefits at a glance, the following comparisons are dated (as I write) and often fail to give critical details, which makes certain comparisons worthless. (Example: one lists the basic cost to publish with CreateSpace as $538. But since you can publish free with Create-Space, which special services are they including? Do the basic costs of other publishers include those features?)

Free comparison of over 100 companies:

http://www.dehanna.com/prntpod.pdf

Free comparison of 30 companies (click on the publisher name and you'll get the basic terms and services and prices of each company):

http://www.booksandtales.com/pod

The Fine Print of Self-Publishing, by Mark Levine (get the most recent edition.) This book compares the contracts of 25 self-publishing companies.

CreateSpace Versus Lulu:

http://crimsonmelodies.com/2011/07/14/createspa
ce-vs-lulu-pod

Compilations of Links on Self-publishing

http://www.sfwa.org/for-authors/writer-beware/pod

http://www.booksandtales.com/pod

Places to Find Complaints

Complaint sites aren't always accurate. Customers have bad experiences with even the best of businesses. And some people complain no matter how great the company is. Thus, every publishing company that's doing a lot of business will have its share of discontents. Sometimes, people with a stake in one company will spread lies about another company.

Yet, although review sites aren't infallible sources of truth, it's important to know what people are saying pro and con. Although people are typically more likely to report bad experiences than good, taken as a whole you find significant differences in the volume and nature of complaints against bad companies and those against good companies. Also, good companies tend to have raving fans who come to the defense of their companies on complaint sites. Before choosing a company, spend some time reading recent customer experiences on sites with no connections to any publisher.

Start by Googling "(publisher name) complaints" or "(publisher name) sucks." Then, simply Google the company's name and see what you find.

Second, visit general complaint sites. Find a search box and type in the name of the company you're checking out.

Better Business Bureau:

http://www.bbb.org

Complaints Board:

http://www.complaintsboard.com

Pissed Consumer:

http://www.pissedconsumer.com

RipOff Report:

http://www.ripoffreport.com

Complaint Now:

http://www.complaintnow.com

(Instead of using the Google Search box on this site, click on the Business link and choose a publishing company in their "Search Business" box.)

* * * * * * *

Note on the Better Business Bureau: The BBB appears to be better in some locations than others. Detractors claim that companies that pay for BBB membership tend to get good ratings, even if they have tons of complaints.

It's at least odd that there's no listing on the BBB site for the Better Business Bureau. In other words, the company that preaches accountability apparently sees no need to allow people to complain about their own company. Weird. Thus, as with any other complaint site, take their recommendations with a grain of salt. (Search Google for "better business bureau complaints" to find news reports on the BBB, the problems businesses are currently having with the BBB, etc.)

The BBB and Publishers: The higher ratings supposedly given to BBB paid members would seem to be impacting their ranking of publishing companies. For example, one self-publishing company has had 284 complaints to the BBB over the past three years, with 38 of the complaints not having been resolved to the customer's satisfaction. Yet, this company pays the BBB to be a member and is thus listed as accredited by the BBB and has an A rating.

Another self-publishing company has only one complaint against it with the BBB for the past three years and it was resolved to the customer's satisfaction. Yet, this company hasn't paid for BBB membership and gets a B- ranking, as well as the notation: "This business is not BBB accredited."

Apple Computers, one of the most successful companies of our time, does not pay for BBB membership and yet has the "This business is not BBB accredited" above its business name, although it gets an A+ rating.

Thus, at this time the BBB is a good place to read complaints and see how companies have responded, but its rating system and accreditation comments can be misleading.

* * * * * * *

Third, check out some publisher specific complaint sites. Again, search the publisher in the search box of each site.

Writer Beware Blogs. A division of the Science Fiction and Fantasy Writers of America, its mission is to "track, expose, and raise awareness of the prevalence of fraud and other questionable activities in and around the publishing industry." Unfortunately, I can't find a search box on the site. A workaround is to type the name of a publisher and the web address in a regular Google search, with "inurl:" or "site:" like this (without the quote marks):

"Publish America inurl:

http://accrispin.blogspot.com "

Whispers and Warnings. Note: This forum is hosted by a self-publishing company, BookLocker, so it may not be entirely objective:

http://forums.writersweekly.com/viewforum.php?f= 14

Forums: With multitudes of authors sharing about their experiences, you quickly learn the difference between publishers' promises and performance. Also, you learn up-to-date changes in policy that are impacting authors.

CreateSpace Community Forum

This specific discussion on the forum gives over 300 replies to the question: "How does Lightning Source compare to Lulu and CreateSpace?"

https://www.createspace.com/en/co
mmunity/thread/3558?start=0&tstart
=0

Since many things have changed since this discussion started in 2008, you may want to start with the most recent replies, which as of today are on this page:

https://www.createspace.com/en/co
mmunity/thread/3558?start=315&tst
art=0

This is a very useful forum, covering multitudes of topics. You may want to search it for discussions concerning Lulu, CreateSpace and Lightning Source.

Helpful Listserv

Sponsored by SPANnet (an open community for independent publishing), the Yahoo *Self Publishing Group* is a lively group of experienced self-publishers who freely share their experiences and opinions. Presently, they're exchanging 500 to 600 messages per month. I've learned much from them.

Helpful Blog Posts and Articles

Aaron Shepherd updates his recommendations with an extensive, detailed article on using LSI and CS, written after Amazon began to list many LSI books as available in 1 to 3 weeks. This reversed his recommendation in his book, *POD for Profit*::

http://www.newselfpublishing.com/PlanB.ht
ml

Joel Friedlander has a lot of wisdom concerning book design and publishing. This post gives critical insights on self-publishing companies. Over 50 replies give valuable experiences on such companies as AuthorHouse, Outskirts, CreateSpace, Lightning Source and Xlibris.

http://www.thebookdesigner.com/2011/05/
subsidy-publishing-proceed-with-caution

Post comparing Lulu with CreateSpace:

Note the following 106 comments as well, which further elucidate people's experiences. Although this was written in 2009, the comments bring the input into 2011:

http://aprillhamilton.blogspot.com/2009/03
/lulu-vs-createspace-which-is-more.html

Good blog post comparing Lulu, CS and LSI:

http://www.blogthority.com/460/cheapest-
self-publishing-comparison-amazon-
createspace-lulu-lightning-press

Writer Beware's "Two Thumbs Down" list of publishers. Over 300 comments both slamming and defending various publishers.

http://accrispin.blogspot.com/2007/02/happy-valentines-day-from-writer-beware.html

OTHER BOOKS BY J. STEVE MILLER

Sell More Books! Book Marketing and Publishing for Low-Profile and Debut Authors: Rethinking Book Publicity after the Digital Revolutions

Can low-profile, not-yet-famous authors get published and sell lots of books? This multiple award winning book says "Yes!" and tells how.

"...a comprehensive guide to marketing a book...[a] well-written, engaging resource that's loaded with specific tips.... Brimming with creative ideas, *Sell More Books!* should prove to be a low-profile author's best friend." - ForeWord Reviews

Social Media Frenzy: Why Time Consuming Facebook, Twitter & Blogging Strategies May NOT Work for Your Business - Consider These Alternative Social Networking Initiatives

How can businesses and individuals harness the power of social media without expending excessive time and effort? Miller contends that in many, if not most situations, the time consuming strategy of trying to build a social media following will waste much time and result in few sales. He supports this position with research and practical examples.

"Solid, well reasoned and sound." – Amazon review.

Enjoy Your Money! How to Make It, Save It, Invest It and Give It: The Adventures of the Counterculture Club

A film producer called it "the money book for people who hate money books." Well researched, but written in story form, this award-winning book makes a great gift for high school and college graduates.

"Had I read this book in my 20's, I'd be financially independent today. It's a remarkable blend of fabulous research with clear and lively writing. You'd pay an expert quite a sum for this caliber of counsel. That's why I say that the best investment you make this year just might be this book. Your second best investment will be the copies you buy for your children." - Dr. Dwight "Ike" Reighard, former Executive Vice President and Chief People Officer, Home-Banc

Near-Death Experiences as Evidence for the Existence of God and Heaven: A Brief Introduction in Plain Language

"For some time we've needed a well-researched, compelling introduction to this exciting field that focuses on the evidence. Miller delivers!" – Jeffrey Long, MD

Reports of near-death experiences (NDEs) are flooding the media with books, articles and interviews. People describe hovering over their bodies, details of their surgeries, talking with deceased relatives, and reviewing their lives in vivid detail, often while their brains should be incapable of producing rational thought or memories.

While the accounts are no doubt interesting, do they provide any solid evidence for the afterlife and the existence of God? Miller argues, in nontechnical and engaging prose, that it does indeed. He began his study doubting that NDEs provided such evidence, but found himself convinced by the weight of the evidence.

Here the reader will explore:

- The common naturalistic explanations for NDEs.
- Evidence that NDEs point to God and heaven.
- The results of 35 years of research into NDEs by doctors and other professionals, fully documented for those who want to study further.
- A comparison of NDEs with Christian teachings.
- Recommendations of key books, researchers, and publications for further study.

"Can we survive death? Is there a God or a heaven? Miller provides the discerning reader with ample reason to think that the answer to these all-important questions is 'yes'." - Dr. Peter Schaefer, Senior Research Psychologist, Department of Defense

Richard Dawkins and His God Delusion: A Preliminary Critique of His Truth Claims

In his best-selling book, *The God Delusion*, Richard Dawkins makes many claims concerning the existence of God and the viability of religion. This brief critique takes several of Dawkins' main contentions and subjects them to research and analysis.

According to Dr. Henry F. Schaefer III, one of the most distinguished living physical scientists, specialist in quantum and computational chemistry, and author of over 1000 scientific publications,

"I welcome this thoughtful and easily digested response to the insubstantial attacks on God by the world's most popular atheist."

About the Author

J. Steve Miller is president of Legacy Educational Resources (www.character-education.info), providing web based resources for those teaching character and life skills in public schools and through service agencies. He and his wife Cherie also write and market their books on various subjects, including their award-winning *Sell More Books! Book Marketing and Publishing for Low Profile and Debut Authors: Rethinking Book Publicity after the Digital Revolutions* , and their personal finance book, *Enjoy Your Money! How to Make It, Save It, Invest It and Give It*. Their sites and blogs now average over 2500 unique visitors (over 7000 page views, 15,000 hits) per day.

Connect with Steve by interacting over Amazon reviews of this book (I comment on Amazon beneath your reviews), or at enjoyyourwriting.com (leave a comment or question, even if it has nothing to do with the post), jstevemiller.com (author site), sellmorebooks.org, Facebook, LinkedIn, and various other blogs, sites and forums.

Made in the USA
San Bernardino, CA
06 June 2013

277569ZR00066

2/13